UP UP!

Jeeva Raghunath

pictures Ashok Rajagopalan

Tulika

Up Up! (English)

ISBN 978-81-8146-567-2

First published in India 2009
Reprinted 2016

Originally in Tamil
English by Sandhya Rao

Published by
Tulika Publishers, 24/1 Ganapathy Colony Third Street, Teynampet, Chennai 600 018, India
email tulikabooks@vsnl.com *website* www.tulikabooks.com

Printed and bound by
Lokavani Southern Printers Pvt. Ltd, 122 Greams Road, Chennai 600 006, India

What is Thumb Thumb Thambi doing?

Thambi takes a piece of paper.

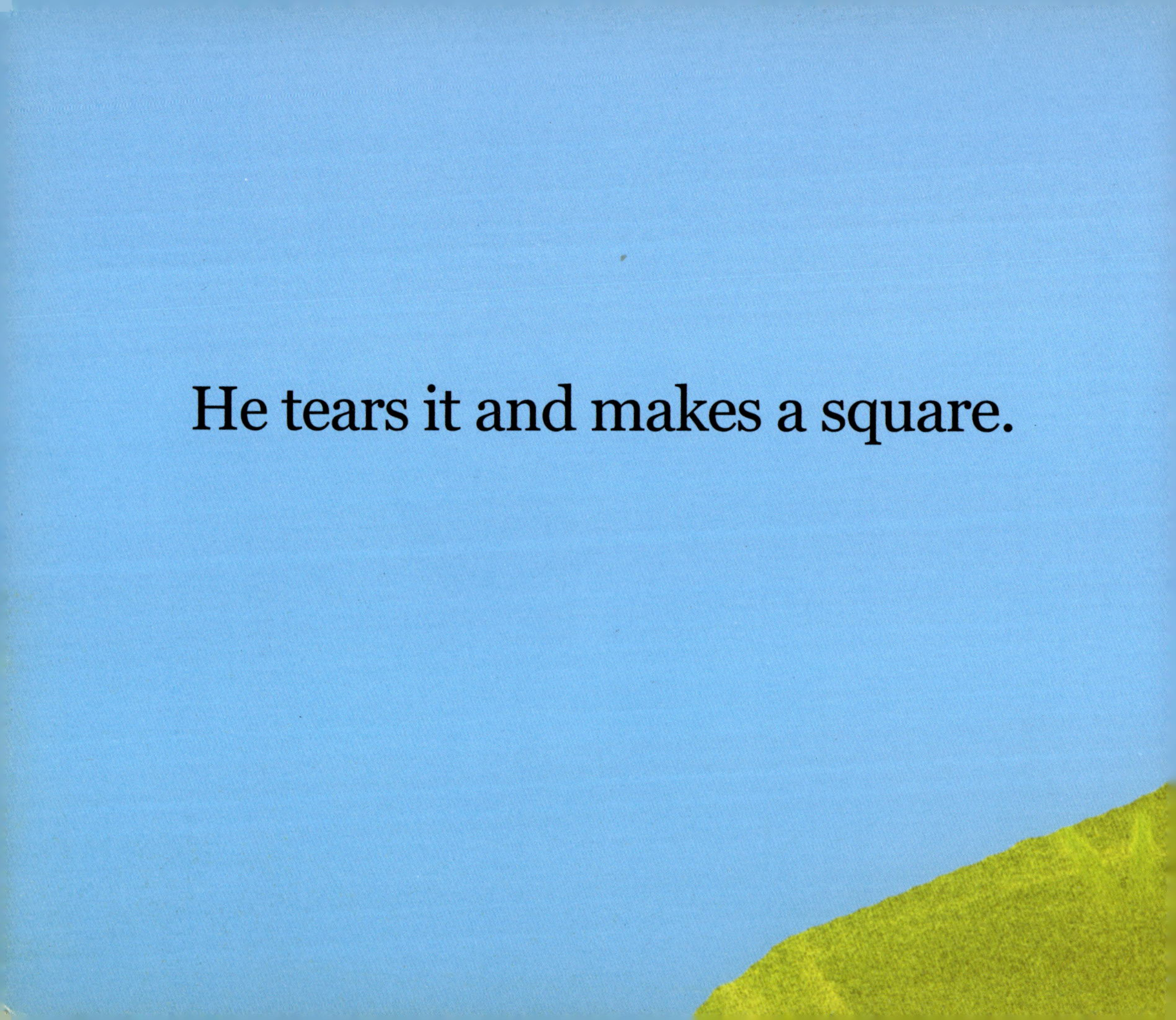

He tears it and makes a square.

He pastes two sticks on it.

He ties a string.

And flies it high in the sky.

The story is over. Let's draw.

This is what Thumb Thumb Thambi sees in the sky.

Put your thumbprint on this page and draw a picture.

This is what I see in the sky.

I CAN READ THIS BOOK!